The Armillary Sphere

The Armillary Sphere

poems

Ann Hudson

OHIO UNIVERSITY PRESS

ATHENS

Ohio University Press, Athens, Ohio 45701
www.ohio.edu/oupress
© 2006 by Ann Hudson

Ohio University Press books are printed on acid-free paper ⊗ ™

14 13 12 11 10 09 08 07 06 5 4 3 2 1

Library of Congress Cataloging-in-Publication Data

Hudson, Ann, 1970–
   The armillary sphere : poems / Ann Hudson.
      p. cm.
   ISBN-13: 978-0-8214-1713-3 (acid-free paper)
   ISBN-10: 0-8214-1713-4 (acid-free paper)
   ISBN-13: 978-0-8214-1714-0 (pbk. : acid-free paper)
   ISBN-10: 0-8214-1714-2 (pbk. : acid-free paper)
   I. Title.
   PS3608.U338A76 2006
   811'.6—dc22

                                                    2006024871

Acknowledgments

My thanks to the following publications where these poems, or versions of these poems, first appeared:

After Hours: "Dream Theory" (as "Dream Theory II"); *Crab Orchard Review:* "The Mobile" (as "The Mobile Maker"); *The Cream City Review:* "The Train"; *Iris:* "Absolute Value," "Berlin Zoo," "Postcard #8"; *Mudfish:* "Oranges"; *Poetry East:* "Grief"; *Prairie Schooner:* "Saint Francis Meets Ella Fitzgerald"; *Re)verb:* "Patron Saint of August"; *The Sow's Ear:* "January 1," "The Miner's Flowers"; *Writing on the Edge:* "Gossip," "Work."

Several of these poems ("The Daughters of Chemical Engineers Understand Chaos," "Schrödinger's Cat," "Laundromat," "Equinox," "Galileo the Clockmaker," "How Glass Is Made," "The Armillary Sphere," "Galileo at Santa Maria Novella") appeared as part of a limited edition chapbook, *Chaos Theory,* by Ultima Obscura Press, 2005.

I wish to thank my teachers, especially Eavan Boland, Rita Dove, Gregory Orr, Jacqueline Osherow, Tom Sellari, Mark Strand, and Charles Wright, for their support and criticism.

I am enormously grateful to Margo Figgins and to the University of Virginia Writers Workshop for showing me what's possible. Thanks to all of my students there and elsewhere for their insight, good humor, patience, and excellent questions.

I am indebted to those who read versions of these poems and made invaluable suggestions, particularly Liz Ahl, Allen Rein, and Margot Schilpp. Thanks to Mary Kinzie for seeing the potential of this book, and to David Sanders, a patient, perceptive, and generous editor, for helping to give it shape. To my friends and family, to Allen, Hannah, Joshua, Barbara, Sarah, and my parents, my deepest thanks for their love and encouragement.

For my mother and father

Wer du auch seist: am Abend tritt hinaus
aus deiner Stube, drin du alles weisst;
als letztes vor der Ferne liegt dein Haus:
Wer du auch seist.

Whoever you are: at evening step forth
out of your room, where all is known to you;
last thing before the distance lies your house:
whoever you are.

from Rainer Maria Rilke's "Prelude"
translated by M. D. Herter Norton

Contents

Patron Saint of August

On Clark Street on a blaze-orange afternoon
the homeless nap in scraps of shade: in doorways,

beneath sun-bleached awnings, between parked cars.
Today you think nothing ever happens here,

not love, grief, gossip; the heat's erased
the possibility of change,

and you've let yourself be dazzled, begging
the daytime moon to let down her silver hair

and rinse you of the heat, but that's just
August talking, just summer sadness. Men

live years riding the El through the city,
or sleeping bundled in U-Haul blankets

beside the lake that feels like a dulled-out ocean,
nickel-gray at dawn and dotted

with gulls. So you avert your eyes
and whistle a tango you've just written,

something you send out to all the people
of this good city, to the patron saint

of August who will keep you moving, moving,
moving past the glassy storefronts,

through the envelope of hazy air,
toward blue waters refreshing as a bruise.

Architect

Are you writing me a poem? my boss asks,
cruising past my desk on his fifth pass of the morning,
looking for work, or signs of working,

of happiness and prosperity, which he might take
for the same thing. He's curious.
Are you building me a house? I ask, barely looking up

from the poem I'm typing on company time,
the phones silent, everyone but the two of us
bent over drafting tables or out for a smoke.

My boss wants what everyone wants:
to be written about. He wants to fill my desk
at work and home. I wonder if he imagines his houses

from the inside out or the outside in,
if he imagines them as a stranger
might admire the beadboard porch ceiling,

the amber lights, the hammered copper mailbox
filled with newsy, beautifully penned notes
from friends with great taste in stationery.

Perhaps he imagines them from the inside,
how a man might take the stairs
two at a time every evening, his hand brushing

the walnut banister in just the same places.
It's my boss's job to know the way morning light
will wake the boy up in his trundle bed,

splashing across his racecar sheets,
or how guests will spill out onto the deck,
margaritas in hand, to check out the view.

It's my job to type his letters, file
his sketches, phone his clients, those people
whose houses he transforms.

It's my job to imagine him imagining a house,
my house, let's say, one with windowsills
deep enough for my ailing houseplants,

a chimney free of birds' nests, and
a sunny corner where I might sit and finish
the poem I started at work this morning when he walked by.

January: Deep Freeze

Because I am tired, because it is the end
of a long week and I feel empty
of anything interesting to say,

I look out the window. So it's at that
moment I catch your eye—you,
walking your ancient mutt, the cigarette

between your chapped fingers
trailing its tiny afterthought of smoke.
It is easy to presume we'll never

meet again, or meet at all, never
exchange a word; it's easy to presume
neither of us will remember this.

It's just as well. In fact, I like
the anonymity, and how I don't
have to ask permission, like it all

almost as much as I like your scruffy
dog, who licks his gray muzzle,
then bites at nothing in the winter air.

Laundromat

Sock to sock, the clothes
match up and collapse
in my hands in neat stacks.
Static fires blue
between the sheets.
It's not a metaphor;
it's a switch of electrons.

The wind is up, it tangles
the honey locust,
tassels the browned azalea blooms.
I smooth each pillowcase
into a regular pane of blue.
Sometimes a man
comes in here to sleep.

Someone calls the police,
but the man's gone
before they get here.
And what's the point?
He doesn't take our keys
or wallets, doesn't steal
a clean shirt from the dryers,

doesn't even speak, just curls
beside the warm machines
and shuts his eyes,
lulled by the regular hum

beneath the thunder. By morning,
when the dark-eyed junco
trills in the honey locust,

he'll be gone.
Twice I've ended up
with socks that aren't mine.
I leave them here.
The weft of wind
beats hard
in the warp of trees.

Galileo at Santa Maria Novella

Ye men of Galilee, why stand ye looking into heaven?

In 1348, it is said,
ten young men and women set out
from this church, and passed
through the great walls of Florence
to escape the plague. The stench
of bodies, sickness, and medicines
was everywhere. Cattle rotted
in the fields. On the journey
the travelers told fantastic stories
of peasants and kings, husbands
and lovers, generosity and betrayal.
Florence dwindled behind them,
its spires receding like the masts
of a drowning ship.

For a hundred nights I have observed
Venus waxing and waning
like our moon. The sun,
not her own body,
is her source of light
as she revolves, like us, around it.
On the thirty-fifth night, Venus appeared
as the curved blade of a silver dagger.
Seven nights passed,
and she swelled to an egg shape.
By shielding my telescope
with a dark glass, I have even seen

irregular bruises on the face
of the boiling sun.

The Holy Spirit intended that the Bible
should teach man how to go to heaven,
not how the heavens go.
Two hundred sixty-six years after the travelers
set out from this church, Father Caccini
stands in its stone archway, squinting in the light.
He denounces mathematics and astronomy
as inconsistent with the holy writings
and as detrimental to the State.
This plague has taken him as well.
His letter is before the Inquisition.
And the sun stood still,
and the moon stayed, until the nation
took vengeance on their enemies.

Midnight: Departure

We park the car at Oceanfront
and 47th, and I follow you
to the beach. I've got nothing new
to say; all I really want
is to walk across the bay, believe
will's more forceful than a riptide.
A mile out, I'd turn, the need
for retrospect too strong, and wave.

Or maybe not. Luck is the shock
of freezing water, to forget all
but the instant, and your body
in it. Shored against the dark,
you watch as I step out, the call
in your opening mouth already empty.

How Glass Is Made

When they reach the rest stop, her father
stretches out beneath the sycamores
and closes his eyes, sending her
and her sisters off to chase each other.
Instead she kneels and asks again
how glass is made. And, like every time,
she never really believes him, though
she's heard about the desert tests,
the heat so fierce there's glass for miles,
and she doesn't understand how sand
can turn so brittle and so clear.
Twice this year her class practiced
filing into the fallout shelter —
the gym, an echoing, cavernous room
that scares her when she's there to play
kickball much less to survive the bomb.
It's always over in fifteen minutes,
and while she sits quietly with her class,
rocking on her heels, glass
is coating the monkey bars and swings,
glazing the parking lot and every
stranded car, encasing people
walking their unsuspecting dogs,
the victims of a Cold War
Vesuvius, statues of the ordinary.

Shapes

A girl sprawls on the sidewalk
as if to swing her limbs in the shape
of a snow angel, though it's October,

Indian Summer, everyone wild
in this last gift of raw, orange light.
Her friend chalks her outline

on pavement confettied with yellow hickory leaves,
then she scrambles up to examine the swollen,
ballooned-up shape of her body.

Soon they're both kneeling and vigorously coloring,
drawing in eyes, lips, hair, like the ancient Egyptians
who figured when you sprang to life from your stiff,

centuries-old pose in the mural, you'd want
all your necessities drawn there with you:
clothes, food, treasures, blessings.

It will only be another few years
before these girls start fasting, try to diet
down a size or two, chew sugarfree gum

for breakfast, laxatives for lunch, hate
the dimples in their thighs, the pucker
around their elbows. Let's hope

they are years away from padded bras,
from fainting spells, from skin
that bruises too easily.

Let's hope these girls remember
this afternoon, the way they plan together
how to draw things in, the marvelous things

their bodies are filled with,
the strong light that extends just beyond
their outreaching fingertips.

But already the storm is rolling in,
pocking the chalk marks.
Rain, its tiny-fingered applause.

Oranges

The summer I turned fifteen
the boy with the most beautiful name
—Carlos, the long avenue

of *oh* through my throat—
picked our orchard. Each year
migrant workers descended on our county

like gypsy moths. In a matter of days
they'd picked the countryside
clean, moved on.

In the long afternoons I watched Carlos
climb the rickety ladder
he fashioned from old crate slats,

watched his body lengthen
with each stretch for the bright fruit,
wrist snapping the orange

from its stem as neatly
as he flicked ash from his cigarette.
As he walked, his hips

swayed slightly in his dirty blue jeans,
boots crusted with fruit rot and mud.
Each night for weeks after he was gone

I'd smell through my open window
the rich, invisible constellations
of oranges in the empty trees.

Night Run

He leads me on a shortcut through the woods,
over two rusted fences slung with barbed wire.

Brambles scratch my bare legs pink
in the November evening cold.

Headlights graze the hemlocks—a month ago
you couldn't see the highway from these woods.

A deer noses into the shadows, flushed out
by hunger. At the foot of a rotting fence post

we find a pine board, painted *Southern Lights, Inc*
and a number. Not a light for miles.

A dog growls as we trot past the long bones
of the silos. Three nights from a full moon,

light glints in warning in the rain-loosened gravel.
My loose, white breath is in my ears.

Kite

Restless sleeper, you slip your hand
beneath my tee shirt, your damp breath
on my shoulder. I was dreaming
of a pond green as apples, of a picnic
in the sweep of trees. So now

I'm more awake than you are, although,
dreaming, you're already pressing
your long body against me. Love takes
more practice than anything.
I can still feel the tug of the kite

in my hands, how we worked
on that hard balance, how much
to pay out, how much to pull,
how to keep it in the wind, aloft,
but keep it. I could let you

ease back into sleep, but why not make love
in the hazy sway and drag of three a.m.,
two flights above the buzzing, green watchfulness
of streetlamps casting shadows
on the ice-slick sidewalks until morning.

Berlin Zoo

In their loamy, half-lit habitat, the marmosets
snatch and pick at their food.
One tiny monkey cocks his head at me,
watches me watch him eat.

Grand Duchess Anastasia loved to come here,
even in the rain, her coat dripping
around her tiny ankles. It was 1922,
seventy years before DNA would prove her

a common Polish worker, not Russian royalty at all.
I grew up only blocks from her
after she moved to the States,
saw her once in the supermarket.

I was nine, going for milk and ice cream
with my father, and she was screeching
and shouting in the frozen food aisle,
swaddled in furs. By then she had over sixty cats,

left milk and tuna on the porch in the August swelter,
and then, when several died, phoned the cops
to report they'd been murdered with arsenic.
Once, when her station wagon broke down

an hour from home, she insisted the car
would have to be towed with her inside.
All the cops knew her. When the tests came back,
some said they knew she'd been a fraud,

knew she'd been faking intimacies
with the royal houses of Europe all along.
I don't think it was an act at all
when she held out her hand to be kissed by visitors,

or when she wandered to the zoo in her amnesiac drizzle,
stood so close to the glass to watch the tiniest
marmoset rolling in the dust, clutching his feet in glee,
that her breath fogged the glass.

I blink. One monkey gnaws the branch he's hanging from,
then scrambles down, lowers his head to his chest
and grooms his belly, as if to say,
Stand there if you'd like—I don't care who you are.

At the Window

Broad daylight, and a man is peeing
against the building across the alley.
The storm is rolling in over the misshapen
skyline. I throw open all the windows.
Rain beads the screens, clogs
the tiny metal mesh. When the storm
has passed, water drains from the lawns,
sun streaks through the soaked trees
in marbled patches, bright draperies
of light decorate the brick apartments.
Outside, in the wet grasses, daffodils
bow in the damp breeze the way a woman
bent over a basin rinses her long, blond hair.

Dream Theory

Copper-orange sunset blazes
through the black branches
of the winter sycamores.
Half-awake, you swear you see
a monarch fluttering in the bookshelf,
its great wingspan the size
of your outstretched hand.
The insect glows as if stained glass,
lit from beneath by its own energy,
by the motion of its flight. The hinge
of its body breathes and trembles,
its great wings shiver open, then
gently fan the air. You've fallen asleep
over the long hinges of open books;
you struggle to wake, to see
the monarch before it escapes.
A suck of darkness, a roar in your ears,
and you slip under, lit by a great flurry
of wings, streaks of copper
and black pressing your lids.

Grief

The kitchen smells like an unwashed
apron. I drift about, pulling
flour, yeast, honey from the shelves.
Under my breath I hum about the sea.
The dough rises as I release
four birds from my sleeves. They fly
to the lights and burst into flames.
I punch down the dough;
it is the color of my skin
and shoulder-smooth. I knead until
someone knocks on the door—
it is my dead mother. She is angry
about the birds, and hands me
a violet feather to swallow. It drags
down my throat, the tiny hairs
tickle. At last it clatters to my stomach
like a dropped coin. It begins to twitch;
I cough, but it is anchored in me
like a bone. It is growing,
tiny wings unfurling, blue flags.

Ode to Julia Child

This is not for every day,
she explains, dipping a crêpe
as delicate as a lady's handkerchief

into the orange sauce and setting it
aflame with brandy.
No, nothing she makes

ever is, not the Apple Charlotte
she made yesterday, soaking
each slice of bread with melted butter

before pressing it in the mold.
Or the Baked Alaska the day before,
the chocolate ganache last week,

and tomorrow, cheese soufflé.
I can't stop watching her assemble
the most heart-stopping foods,

everything a triumph of excess:
soup with a pint of whole cream,
lemon poundcake with a half-dozen eggs.

Forty years ago, my mother
was a bride in a tidy house
under a midwestern sky as flat

as a cast-iron skillet.
No gourmet chef, my mother,
but good at invention. She watched Julia

on a tiny black-and-white TV,
laughed to see a chef pick dropped food
off the counter and return it

to the bowl with a simple
They'll never know the difference.
See, Julia knows that the proper way

to make a meal is to taste it as you go along,
use only the finest ingredients,
and throw in whatever seems best:

raisins in the casserole,
balsamic vinegar in the savory pie.
If every day we ate like this,

spooning cream sauces and desserts
into our pink and open mouths,
wouldn't we live like kings?

And who better to rule us
than a queen liberal with the wine,
the finest threads of saffron, and the rules?

Gossip

It bites back, like the jay
in the overgrown azalea who
digests all the afternoon songs

and cackles them back again,
topping it off with his own
queedle-queedle.

I'm sick of him today,
tired of being drawn to the window
to search him out in the deep foliage,

tucked and bobbing
in the flicking leaves.
My students have, I've heard,

paired me off with half the teachers
at the school, have dissected
what they've guessed and what I've told them

of those brief hours from mid-afternoon
until just after dawn when we all
materialize at the classroom door again.

They know I've been up to something
all that time—drugs, or running drugs
across the border, petty theft, public

nudity. I'm the next toy
come to life, after the doll they dressed
and undressed with their friends,

Barbies they twisted into flat,
un-organed sex with plastic Ken,
then abandoned, naked,

in the Dream House to sleep it off,
wiser and looser in the joints.
It must feel daring to invent

such a secret life for someone who seems
more likely to take an interest in parts of speech
than parts of the body, in variables

other than love, or sex. Leaves twitch,
the jay is safely tucked in a scramble of foliage.
He screams the shrill cry

of the red-shouldered hawk.
Why not practice on someone you can watch all day,
and disassemble?

First Day of Spring

It's a wild March morning in Chicago, the wind
dragging its nets through the streets,
trawling for its usual and plentiful treasures:

crushed styrofoam cups, torn newspapers,
lost gloves, a blizzard of fast food napkins.
I take my eight-year-old Toyota

through the car wash. Idling in neutral,
I ease past the powerful, shaggy brushes,
the nozzles spraying limp foam onto the hood,

and remember the sick excitement I felt
when my father took my sisters and me through,
all the windows of our '67 baby blue Valiant

tightly cranked, the antenna pushed into its sleeve,
our doors locked against who-knows-what,
the three of us with our identical haircuts

buckled into the back seat, our identical shoes
drumming the vinyl. I was sure
those huge blue brushes would crash

right through the windshield and pin us to our seats.
At eight, a child sure of impending danger, this
was about all the thrill I could handle.

I pull out of the car wash into the tangle
of traffic, past the bars that open at nine in the morning
and stay open, past the disheveled and pacing junkies,

past the crumbling theater draped in shadow and disrepair,
and make slow headway against the wind
that gathers the stray grocery bags all over the city,

whipping them against the masts
of budding hawthorns, silver maples,
bald cypress, green ash, green ash.

Insomnia

If you were awake too, I'd tell you
the whole story, how I dreamt
we never saw the child, how easily

we forgot. Instead I shuffle
to the porch to watch
traffic pass the house,

and an occasional bat dive
under the streetlamps, ruthless
after its dark targets.

The Train

The woman stitches the mouth of a buttonhole.
Her fingers ripple the thin cloth.

The train streaks through wheat fields, past farms
knotted along the Elbe, heads south along the river,

still three hours from Berlin, only an hour
left of light. The woman's needle pierces,

the thread hisses through. In Hamburg, a man's
translucent-blue body was dragged from the river.

Water drained from his nostrils; his watch, clasped
to his porcelain-blue wrist, still ticked.

The woman glimpses her reflection
in the blue-black glass, quick hands

darting back and forth. She feels the pull at her dress,
barely sees her face, a glass dinner plate.

Schrödinger's Cat

Here's how it works: if I don't call
for the results of my blood test
the answer might be yes, it might be no,

but it's mine to guess, and perhaps
not knowing's a fair price to pay
for this uneasy stillness, all possibilities

still alight. So instead I creak open
the screen door for the stray,
feed her some dry food I keep

beneath the sink so the landlord
won't notice, then stroke the creature
as long as she permits before she scuttles

to my study, pokes her head
into the overflowing closet, circles twice
and flops unceremoniously on the rug

to take a nap. Her lower jaw
quivers, her paw twitches
and unsheathes its claws. Her tail flicks,

deep breaths fill her soft belly and chest.
One eye closed, one half open,
its winking membrane barely

sliding open like a reception window,
and the voice behind it asks,
Is it yes or is it no?

Saint Francis Meets Ella Fitzgerald

It's early evening, the stars
just clicking on in the spangled vaults

of heaven. A fine sheen
of sweat glistens the cocktail glasses.

Tonight, like every night, the cover charge
is minimal, and the view

is outstanding. Small talk,
like music, is all about improvising

on a known quantity: the weather,
the family, the recessed murals

which everyone understands
conceal secret passageways.

Decked out in a robe of sparrows,
Francis gets a bead on the woman

receding into the shadows.
The bird-guy smiles at her shyness,

and threads his way across
the crowded room. As if on cue,

Gabriel steps up for a solo,
arching so far back

his rosy robes sweep the horizon.
Francis gently guides her by the elbow

to the microphone. As her song
unravels from her throat he thinks,

Lord, make me an instrument,
and means just that.

Work

Twelve students cram
around the folding table, two
slump on the nearby sofa.
All have been sober or clean
at least thirty days. Thirty days ago
I got my hair cut, did laundry,
nothing of much consequence,
while they made a new deal
with their bodies, smoked packs,
slept, left friends who use.
Today I set them writing.
They can't sit still; they tip back
in their chairs, throw pens across the table,
speak whatever comes
to mind whenever it comes.
The two boys on the couch
have pulled the afghan over themselves
and are pretending to have sex, moaning
and grinding. Others call out for gum,
show off their pierced tongues.
Eric, after announcing it's been
three days since he slept
then burping loudly, grins sunnily
and looks at his paper, scribbles.
For whatever reason his movement
catches on, and Bill bends his shorn head
over his work; Holly, each nail adorned

with a miniature seascape
complete with palmtree and sky,
writes her name across her empty page.
How obsessed they are with the body:
farts, sex, snot, hunger, thirst, piss,
shit, hard-ons . . . What work it takes
to grow up into your own body, to come
clean with it, to get dirty with it,
to live peacefully inside it as if
that were the most natural thing in the world.

The Daughters of Chemical Engineers
Understand Chaos

Evenings, our tall fathers come home muttering,
mulling over the latest data, looking for the big picture,
the practical application. On the backs of papers
with endless equations that our fathers read
like sheet music, we crayon houses, flowers,
the sun as bright as a nickel in the corner of the page,
the double curve of birds above the trees.
Our fathers murmur into their plates
while we twirl spaghetti in tightening spirals,
flecking our white tee shirts with constellations
of marinara. Our fathers cut their dinners in neat grids,
carefully savoring each tidy, square mouthful. ·

Absolute Value

Morning sun freckles the city river.
In the storefront window, beneath
the ornate clock as big as a whale's eye,
a woman polishes a bare mannequin
with a cucumber-green sponge,

scrubbing the sternum with such vigor
I wince. What I at first mistake for grime
are hollows at the mannequin's shoulders
and pubic bones. The empty bowl of her pelvis
tilts toward me in the glittering window.

She's supposed to look young, I think,
just like my friend who has checked herself
into yet another hospital, her skin
as dingy as a gym towel. She's taking
math to heart, measuring herself

by absolute value, how far she is from zero.
Once I was there to see her off, waited
with her for the ambulance flashing up the drive.
She whispered how it felt to skydive,
the parachute blooming from her narrow shoulder blades,

how she had to wear a weighted suit to bring her down.
Without it, how long would she have drifted,
kiting over farmlands in eerie silence?
A peninsula of trees extended like an olive branch
as if she were anchored to anything in this world.

Postcard #8

From out west my cards are slow to reach you.
I think of them on their long trip
across the continent, each a tiny, colorful lie.

Actually, I've never seen the Great Salt Lake at night
as my earlier card announced, but one late afternoon
I walked the salt flats, briny air burning my lungs.

High over the train transformed into a gift shop,
the unlikely shapes of inland seagulls skimmed and dived,
sketching, in the dimming light, illusory maps

that wouldn't guide you back to where I'm watching
the sunset make a stranger landscape, painting shore
and water the colors salt makes when thrown in fire.

What We Throw Away

He looks so small to be crawling in the dumpster,
one leg dangling like a half-damaged scarecrow's
out of the side opening. One morning

he scared me half to death as I walked
to my car in the pre-dawn chill.
I didn't hear him, he rummaged so quietly

among the sour foods, the stained grocery bags of trash.
Suddenly we were eye-to-eye, my hand on the car door,
his clutching torn jeans he'd salvaged from a bag.

My neighbor jokes that he's our building's own
recycling program, since each morning he carts off
the cans and bottles we've ignored.

How surprised he'll be to find the gun
you nestled in an enormous box of styrofoam packing
beneath a rusty folding chair. The clip

you hid in a dumpster down the street,
then each of seven bullets in a different trash can.
You're as meticulous about avoiding death

as you are about dying, tracing each step
in the evening drizzle as cleanly as you snap
the clip in place. I didn't talk you out of it;

you simply changed your mind.
Tonight, the night you didn't die,
I wash each dinner plate twice, then go to bed

even before it's dark. Squirrels thump in the dumpster,
chitter on the great limbs of the elm outside my window,
chuck nuts into the bushes below. By the time

I wake he'll be back again, hunting for what
we've missed in our marred sights:
some trace of food, clothing, safety.

February Morning: First Trimester

Before I've pulled the key
free from the lock the puppy
is at my ankles; he snuffles the hem
of my coat, then leaps to lick my hand.
Before I can bend to pet him
or check his collar for tags,
he sprints to a neighbor's stoop to nip
at the morning paper in its blue sleeve
then scampers half a block away
and back again, barking with joy
at all the overcoated commuters
striding to the train. The same moment
that I realize no one is tending
to this rambunctious dog, he spots
a well-behaved retriever on a leash
and darts across the busy street.
I flinch at the squeal of brakes,
but with the luck of the very young
and foolish, this puppy, somehow
suddenly *my* puppy, misses
the oncoming car by inches
and doesn't seem to notice,
barely glancing back at me as I
take off after him, so happy is he
with his new game until I tackle him
in the alley. He struggles in my arms,
his thrashing, muscular body

straining to race away. Blind force.
His only questions are who to trust,
from whom to kick free, and
how long to run.

The Armillary Sphere

One warm evening a man and woman play
in the park on toys named
for their imperatives: *slide, swing*. Bats

swoop through the broad limbs
of the cottonwoods, toward the last
rung of light over the distant, glittery lake.

With broad strokes the pendulums
of the chain-stitch swings cross
and cross in cadence in the dark.

She leans back in her seat like the woman
in Brueghel's *Allegory of Air*
who half-reclines on a gray rock

encircled by a fantastic throng of birds:
peacock, heron, turkey, dove. To one side
a crooked branch spokes from the ground,

glittering with songbirds. Behind her, Apollo
sails through the breaking clouds
in his golden chariot drawn by four restless horses,

but he's even smaller than the peacock, the tapestry
spread at her feet. The Pleiades
pin themselves in her hair; her body shines

with soft light. In her fingers rests a globe
of gold bands: an armillary sphere
which calculates the elevation of the sun.

Apollo would never know how high he flew,
unless he accidentally slid too near the ground
and scorched the grass and trees. Perhaps

she's the little-known goddess of astronomy,
or just a dabbler, watching Apollo trace his exact,
predetermined passage through the heavens.

Though Apollo must illuminate her back, oddly
it's the front of her that's lit.
Maybe we all have two sources

of light, the more conspicuous god-driven,
a white thunder of hooves, the other
a still ladder of birds, a lake, the outlying shore.

Charge

In her favorite black-and-white
they're stepping into the new darkness,
ducking beneath a spray of sparks
friends hold out to bless them with,

a crackling umbrella of electric charge.
Blurred out, backlit in the arched doorway,
their mothers watch them make their way
away. Dazzle of sparks in the foreground,

the soft empire of darkness and family
behind . . . The row of sparklers arch
like flying buttresses to shore them up,
their faces tilted to the crystallized light.

Eurydice

Why follow him out of the kingdom,
and back into what? A world
where she'd lose children to illness, accident,
the whims of the gods? She'd have to admit
she was relieved to have her husband's faithlessness
proven to her once and for all. She'd even
tiptoed along behind just to unnerve him,

having learned quite well the walk of the dead.
He never could keep her birthday gifts secret,
always gave them to her a few days early
because he couldn't stand the suspense. Really,
it was easy, more than easy even; the poor guy
didn't stand a chance. She thought she'd mind
the guilt of his unhappiness, but it was

the first time he took his responsibility
to heart. After all, he'd been dallying
with pretty girls for years, some groupies
he'd met at gigs, even some of her closest
friends. He'd blamed it all on her, of course,
her aging body, the paunch of her belly
that had borne three children they both

truly loved. She'd miss them, but really,
it was better this way. She'd spend
the rest of time with them, and once her eyes

refocused in the dark, it wasn't half bad.
Perhaps a tad cool for her sunny tastes.
She smiled sadly as she turned away from him.
After everything, she was the one to leave.

The Mobile

Imagine this dream:
late afternoon sun lights it
as if from inside,

glowing it bronze, glowing it
apricot, glowing it rose. It moves
like a woman chasing sandpipers

along the tide line. It glows
like a train of thought,
like a lighthouse at the bottom of the sea.

In the empty room, it
twirls slowly, like a girl who
watches the silhouette

of her dress in the reflection
of a shop window; it moves
like a woman who,

putting away a clean glass,
pauses to watch her hand,
which though not pretty is

a hand she loves. The mobile moves
quietly and with great, dark
joy in the room,

in the room with light
lowering down the walls like water
draining from a glass.

Imagine this creature in a slow
spin, its skin as smooth
as cream swirling in coffee,

sandpipers skimming the waves.
Imagine that nothing
is more remarkable, not even

the scraps of discarded tissue
on the tile, not the red,
muscular heap on the floor,

bright as a lollipop,
not the fibrous muscles, organs,
the white spine.

The sandpipers startle;
you wake, and a long rope
of birds rises over the water.

Galileo the Clockmaker

As a boy in Pisa I watched a monk
draw the cathedral chandelier toward him
with a pole, touch his torch to each wick,
then let the great lamp swing away.

Light swept the stone floor, a gold medallion.
No matter how long the stroke of the pendulum,
while it swung, it measured the same time
with each arc. A monk flourished a censer,

the strong perfume ascending
in ornate loops toward the steepletop.
When news of my spyglass reached Venice,
I was summoned before the Senate.

Many of the nobles insisted they climb,
wheezing and coughing, the steepest church tower
to observe the ships that nearly two hours later
steered full-sail into their harbor.

I returned to my study to watch the moon
glide along heaven's sphere as regularly
as a nun's fingers moving
along the circle of her rosary.

Ill, my sight dimming, I dictate the design
of my new clock to Vincenzio.
The moon wheels all night across his sketches.
We race to finish, my fingers trembling

over the gearwork and the pendulum
that drives the great wheel forward.
The senators say it's impossible, but I know
it can be done. Even a blind boy fumbling

inside a burning house feels which way
the fire comes for him, the mark of heat
on his skin more accurate
than sight in the smoke-filled room.

Equinox

It is believed by most that time passes; in actual fact, it stays where it is.
— Zen master Dogan

Sycamores in bloom, and still more new leaves
unfurl, green as antifreeze.
Cicadas buzz like antique refrigerators.

We shift ahead another year, our shadows
longer and longer. We try to downsize,
slough off old clothes, bad books,

mementos we nest our houses with
to anchor us to where we've been.
It doesn't matter that this never works.

We can't even stand still without conversion,
turning out cells like new leaves,
the carousel of seasons tilting above us.

From a shrub, two sparrows fly up
in a double helix and dart away.
We repeat ourselves endlessly

and are never the same.
Forecast: clouds
and persistent rain, persistent rain.

After Dark

A slow rain blankets the house.
From the kitchen, voices drift
up the darkened stairs. I practice witchcraft,
willing my attic room into Atlantis,

raising from the abyssal ocean plains
vibrant masses of anemone and coral.
Moonlight drains off the ruined walls of the cathedral
I've drawn back up on land. The waxy stains

of green and yellow crayons on my lampshade
throw an eerie map of shadow
on the wall, disguising my sheets and pillow.
Continents drift around my bed.

My mother kisses me goodnight as carp
and lanternfish swim toward me in half-sleep.

Insomnia

By midnight it's clear
it's too humid to sleep,
so I drag a chair to the open window.
Magnolia blossoms unfold, fragrant
as burnt sugar. City lights
glint in the distance.

The full moon rises over the valley,
the dull gold of my grandfather's watch.
He's been dead a dozen years, but in the garden
his spearmint still comes up wild.
Katydids croon from the osage orange.

I wake to find his pocket watch
under my pillow. It leaves a bruise
on my jaw as round and dark
as a beetle. I move through the rooms
without speaking, the mark ticking
all morning, all afternoon.

The Miner's Flowers

Miles of tunnels twist beneath
this town, this green yard, this boy
swinging above the white violets.

The air is sweet with rotting walnuts.
Bud-laced branches diagram
his name in the blank sky.

In a canary hard hat his grandfather
whistles tunelessly down a mineshaft
while carts rattle past

with peaks of bluish gray ore.
He squints at a half-rotting beam overhead.
Twice last August their house

was struck by lightning—
the clocks stopped, and their mouths
tingled as they ran to the yard,

but nothing ever caught fire.
At the end of summer they posed
for a photograph on the porch

for luck. The miner turned to watch
his son lift the boy in his arms,
a blue pinwheel in his chalky hand.

January 1

To do anything daily, beyond the simple
urgencies of the body, beyond the claims
of job or family, to volunteer
for daily work: the metallic sweat
of exercise, meditation, or
an appreciation of the linden tree
twenty steps from your office, the one that spreads
its generous boughs like a giant octopus,
like a wide-brimmed hat you wear
to shade your faded blue eyes from the wintery sun
when you look up, humming, at its upper
branches, your scarf loosening in the long wind,
shade blading your throat. Every day.